comet scar

ALSO BY JAMES HARMS

What to Borrow, What to Steal
After West
Freeways and Aqueducts
Quarters
The Joy Addict
Modern Ocean

Limited Editions and Chapbooks
Double Nickels on the Dime
East of Avalon
L.A. Afterglow

comet scar

poems by
James Harms

Carnegie Mellon University Press
Pittsburgh 2012

Acknowledgments

My thanks to the editors of the following journals and anthologies where the poems in this book first appeared, often in earlier versions and occasionally with different titles:

Barrelhouse ("Bachelor Kisses"), *The Blue Moon Review* ("So Long, Sunset Boulevard"), *Burnside Review* ("The Shield (of Captain America)"), *Cave Wall* ("Another," "Flags," "Though Not about Him or for Him, a Poem Called Bill Murray"), *Cerise Press* ("Or Two Cans Tied Together with String"), *The Cincinnati Review* ("Phoebe"), *Colorado Review* ("Range Life"), *Connotation Press* ("Making Up for Lost Time," "Providence"), *Crazyhorse* ("Boundary Rider," "Lynda (Singing Chet Baker, 1988)," "Lost and Through"), *Drunken Boat* ("Black Mule," "You the Overheard"), *The Gettysburg Review* ("Cary Grant"), *Gulf Coast* ("The Clock"), *The Laurel Review* ("It's OK if He's a Girl"), *Oxford American* ("Murmur R.E.M."), *Pebble Lake Review* ("Bar Talk, "First Day of Spring"), *Poetry International* ("Friday Rich/Saturday Poor," "In Your Bright Ray," "My Life in Art"), *Poetry Southeast* ("Song of Sand, Song of Sea, Song of Leaving, Song of Leaves"), *Quarterly West* ("Lamp by Lamp," "School Figures"), *Sycamore Review* ("The Astronaut"), *Tygerburning* ("A Wooden Horse"), *Valparaiso Poetry Review* ("Keep My Word"), *West Branch* ("Comet Scar," "March 17th," "We Started Home, My Son and I").

"Antarctica Starts Here," "Gypsy Hollow," "Satie," and "Trapped" appeared in the chapbook *Double Nickels on the Dime*, published by *The Idaho Review*. My thanks to Mitch Wieland.

"We Started Home, My Son and I" was reprinted in the 2007 *Pushcart Prize XXXII*. "Song of Sand, Song of Sea, Song of Leaving, Song of Leaves" was reprinted in *Bear Flag Republic: Prose Poems from California*. "Bar Talk" was reprinted in the *Alhambra Poetry Calendar 2009*. "Lamp by Lamp" was reprinted in the *Alhambra Poetry Calendar 2011*.

My gratitude to the National Endowment for the Arts for a fellowship that supported the writing of some of these poems, and to the writers, painters, musicians, architects, actors, dancers and friends who populate (and inspired) many of the poems in this book.

Thanks also to the Eberly College of Arts and Sciences at West Virginia University for its longstanding support.

The following poems take their titles and inspiration from songs by Grant McLennan, 1958-2006, and were written in his memory: "Bachelor Kisses," "Black Mule," "Boundary Rider," "The Clock," "Comet Scar," "First Day of Spring (The Day My Eyes Came Back)," "In Your Bright Ray," "Keep My Word," "Lamp by Lamp" and "Providence."

Library of Congress Control Number 2011926146
ISBN 978-0-88748-546-6
Copyright ©2012 by James Harms
Printed and bound in the United States of America

10 9 8 7 6 5 4 3 2 1

Contents

FOR AMANDA

How can we imagine what our lives should be
without the illumination of the lives of others?

—JAMES SALTER, *LIGHT YEARS*

ONE

We Started Home, My Son and I

after Jaan Kaplinski

We started home, my son and I.
Evening beginning. The small stains
of streetlight spreading across the sidewalk,
thinning to darkness every few yards.
My son paused at the edge of each
then leapt, one hand in mine,
to the next. Ahead, his mother
touched the meat twice before
turning it, rinsed the lettuce, called out
for his sister to wash her hands.
He said each spot of light
was a great land, each span
of darkness the sea. And we
followed his map home
out past the edge of town where night
filled the long blocks between
streetlights with oceans.
We rowed when we could, swam
the last few miles. Until the moon
reared up like an old man
startled from his nap. And once
again the roads of the world rose
beneath us. Before long, my son
and I were home. I watched him climb
the brick stairs to the front door,
whose key I no longer owned.
His mother waved as he fell
into the house, the bright rooms
splashed with light. The ottoman
covered with horsehair; a damask
draped over the sofa: I couldn't see
these or any other emblems of my
previous life. I felt the waters rise
around my feet, heard in the distance

the loose rigging in the wind, a buoy bell.
So far from the sea, I rolled up
my trousers, wading in
for the walk back.

Boundary Rider

Grant McLennan, 1958-2006

The fence holds back
the cattle, the cane just beyond and beyond
that a field of waste where husks
and cinders shift and spark in the wind,

where a boy walks home from school
through flakes of ash rising
like snow shadows into cloud. As much
as it retrieves, memory unmakes.

It lifts the cinders back to air
and finds the lost watch
in the shower; his father always left it
on the dresser with his change, his cigarettes.

The dead are like yesterday's forgotten
umbrella, equally real
to time, like the smell of coffee
in a field of burning cane.

But the boy doesn't need to remember, not yet,
balanced on the fence and
strolling post to post
like a counter of calves.

Is this the waste of memory or something saved,
the lost tooth wrapped in foil
and sealed with a slip of paper
in a sandwich bag ("Grant's first, 1964")?

From post to post a man rides and names
the cattle he can't keep in, the memories
he can't keep out. His father watches
from a hill dissolving in the heat.

How much is it worth,
the scent of sea on the wind,
the leaves caught like worn lunch bags
on the barbed wire laced between beams?

How much the smell of coffee
in a field on fire, a watch wound
too tight and ticking cut time?

And here's a stripe of sunlight in a voice
half-hidden by music in the mangroves.

And here's a box of song instead of ash.
We lift the lid and let you go.

My Life in Art

She felt the edges of the moment like the smooth face of a dime.
I felt her face with my eyes closed against the sparks, the spray
around her fingers as she opened an orange.

She guessed about my money. She showed me the buttons on
     the inside.

For hours the rain thickened into snow then back again.
She said, OK, enough, just talk about your brother,
the last good wave you caught before leaving but don't

don't do that. But she let me. The clasp

is what I'd call it. A hook, she said, and I had it in my teeth
as she lit a cigarette and said, It's snow now for good.
We heard the same small voice become a crocus in the earth

beside the path, a car in the cough descending the staircase.

You can't afford this, she said. Or that. I showed her
     my fake eye,
my blond marble, my wallet photo of Katherine Ross
     as Etta Place.
She sang instead of anything, though she held me a while,

or part of me. And when I floated away I left a gift in her hand.

A little pearl.

Friday Rich / Saturday Poor

The swans follow Helen, a sandwich
in her pocket. And now she's screaming
at her boyfriend, "Thank you
for making me beg," as he rides away
on his Schwinn waving one finger.
Beneath the bridge the smell of batteries
and goose shit, the smell of old wool
all wet with fog and breath, the smell of
Friday night, the smell of clear air beaten
blue by spray paint and rotten fruit.
Even Hector has a check to cash
and we're all wondering where
to go first: the liquor store
on Beechurst or the sub shop
near the bus station. I wish
Helen's phone would stop ringing.
I never understand the river town girls
with their frayed sleeves
and pearls like broken teeth
around their necks, at their wrists.
If we hurry we can spend every dollar
by dawn. The smell of iron
or the taste of it. The look of Helen
all stoned and happy in a
gas lamp's gold glow. The look
of beer in a glass. The look
of polished wood, the ring stains
and puddles, the letters carved
with a penknife: "Friday
is a kiss." I don't get the steam
on the river. I wish the moon
would stop shaking. I wish Saturday
would stay still on the other side
of midnight. There's a little girl or Helen
staring at a shop window,
waiting for the mannequin to move.

Flags

Apparently we didn't have a song.
"Kind of Blue," "Blue Stranger,"
"Blue Hotel," "Blue Spark," "Blue
Monday," "When the Stars Go
Blue" . . . take your pick, I said.
I remember being dipped in honey
and staked to the anthill: beats Orpheus
and the Maenads, but that's about it.
I had a view of mountains as daylight
drained down the hollows and coulees
and turned to blue in the sea.
I heard their little jaws creaking, the ants,
but except for that, being eaten alive
is not at all like divorce. My neighbor
is all about flags, hoisting Old Glory
every morning, folding her up at dusk:
sometimes I help him get the corners
neat on his triangle of stripes.
He has a porch flag for every holiday
though he's giving up on St. Patrick:
"March is brutal on flags," he says, mopping
his brow with stars. He started
his own cemetery on the knoll behind
the elementary school, in sight of
anyone on the anthill, which is how I know
he's burying more than our neighbors.
There's protocol for disposing of flags,
a hymn to whistle as the children
accelerate in a circle, but I'm tired of choking
on radio waves, of waking full of
someone else's song: "Sweet sunshine
in a pail, the wind in a cup, the lemonade
is free, so you better drink up."
I used to wonder a lot about the atmosphere,
how much speed it takes to break through
the sky, what angle is best, etc. But I was wrong

about the rags, or rather flags, wrong
that they weren't rolled up with ash,
the box smoking with the recently departed.
I met a girl who tuned herself like a radio
to those flecks of sound no one can see
or hear, though we breathe them. Which is why
you find yourself whistling for no good
reason, not a graveyard in sight, a song
rising up through your body like ash
in the wind, like smoke. I used to watch
the smoke come out of her ears just before
the tears. There are always at least two methods
for registering rage, dozens for loss.

Phoebe

She's listing the leaves again.
She's beginning with leaf
like a hand, then
leaf like a little leaf.
She's folding the leaf
like a letter into a map
to fit in her pocket.
The letter begins,
Dear Me, How are you
but I already know.
She's licking a lemon
plucked from my tea,
the glass on a tray on
the porch steps.
She's shaking a spoon
of wet sugar.
She's lecturing a year-old
nest finally fallen
from the elm, saying
How could you? She walks
the nest to a pile of leaves;
she buries it deep, she digs it out.
She spends fifteen minutes
trying to throw it back
into the tree before
she looks at me again,
before anything else.

Or Two Cans Tied Together with String

1.

My wife sings like laughing
water in a pot, peels
onions for a stew that will
by evening's end simmer with
the old earth smells of lamb and
rosemary, potatoes and saffron,
all other scents just quiet clamor
in the steam leaking out
the open window above the sink,
where minutes ago she
gathered in the bird and kissed
the gray down of its neck
before tugging loose the note,
before returning it to the air.

2.

I fell asleep mid-afternoon
and woke to bells and the dusty tin
notes of an antique piano, flurries
aging the early evening. I made
a sandwich of mustard and cheese,
stood at the window watching
the music blow with snow
in the back yard, wrapped
a Chinese fortune around my last
pigeon's rickety left leg
and climbed the rope ladder
to the roof to let it go.

3.
Once I hid a love note
in her sock drawer and waited
months until she found it.
By then nothing had changed.
Which is a way of saying love
is a glacier devouring the daisies
in a mountain meadow:
they disappear so slowly
we forget to remember the beauty.

4.
I slid the cold pigeon inside
my shirt before returning it
to the cage. My wife was
singing "Ruby Mae," the window
still cracked enough to let out the song
with all that steam, the sounds
beneath the smells, how a voice
changes over time and distance.
Or it doesn't.

Bar Talk

(The Magnificent Grill, Morgantown, WV)

Bits of bullet, the shards and stains, boots full
of blood, the walking around on bones, the knife
and razor shaving years from each edge of a perfect life,
the spent wisdom, the nods and shrugs and willful
giving up on going on: so what? He was right,
whoever he was who rang down the night
like a hand clapped to a shoulder, a forearm,
a balled fist shivering on the table top, the bar,
the jukebox full of Jackson Browne, the Eagles, the Dead;
he was right: "Figuring it all out is the ass end
of memory, is why you're here instead of sleeping
with her hair half in your mouth, your breath
half-gone, choking on her and happy to, a little death.
So now you know what's what, that easy feeling,

peaceful. Well, let me introduce you to tomorrow."

Satie

Between Walt's scab and the corner
tobacconist is a purple plywood airplane
in someone's backyard and three brushstrokes
by de Kooning circa 1983, a single day
turned into ribbons of red and blue, the blue
now and then scraped down to white
or a shadow of buried yellow,
morning in Springs. Or morning in Morgantown,
where Joni Mitchell spent a season
listing reasons to leave until *his*
name appeared on the page (shh: Jackson Browne).
Who else is buried at Springs?
Walt fell while being chased on the playground
and keeps losing his Band-Aid,
which is like breathing heat into cupped
hands until you're dizzy and spinning
in flurries at afternoon's end.
De Kooning forgot his name
but not the moment his wrist should turn
and end the stroke, the easing of
pressure as the brush softened
to air and a few bristles then nothing,
though he stood there for hours so full
of forgetting the canvas began
to dry. Walt says, "One more Band-Aid, please,"
as Amanda dabs Neosporin with a finger,
now smudging with her thumb
to keep the scab from cracking, from
starting to bleed again. I'm off
to the corner for more Band-Aids and
cigarettes, and to see if anyone's
won the Lotto. What to whistle
when the weather calls for "*Je te veux*"
but all I've got on my iPod is
If You're Feeling Sinister? Oh, well (shrug):
"Like Dylan in the Movies." Good enough.

Song of Sand, Song of Sea,
Song of Leaving, Song of Leaves

"Here Comes a Regular," Balboa Pier

I own this song like a buffalo nickel, carry it around to offer
the air every day or two when I'm alone in the garden, the
shower.

*

And now it drifts through the parking lot and out beneath the
pier, a bit of musical tulle fog lapping at beach towels, a song so
secret I'm sad to hear it leak from a low-slung El Camino.

*

The bubbling edge of a broken wave is singeing Walt's ankles,
his first time by the sea.

*

Beyond him a line of pelicans shoots the pier heading north,
wings wide and still in the inch of air above water; Walt turns
to yell, mouth full of wind, his words torn apart by the wake of
Pacific waves.

*

The El Camino leaves the parking lot and leaves behind my
song of leaves: *First the lights then the collar goes up, the wind
begins to blow. . . . First the past then the leaves that last, here comes
the snow.*

*

Catalina floats in the deeper distance like a cloud settling on
the water as Walt breads himself with sand, rolling toward the
ocean, singing.

*

I walk down to the water to hear his new voice, changed by the
sea, to help him wash the beach off his body.

*

And Walt wants to know did I see the birds.

*

And Walt wants to splash me, the cold Pacific: he's laughing
and so am I, each of us someone's, each of us fearless, within
reach.

School Figures

after Machado, with a line from Levis

Someone said light means everything
it cannot say,
which is a way
of excusing the flash of sound
released from a fist
hammering an empty desk,
or the way a word wavers like heat
in the middle distance
of a classroom, the students reciting
their 3's, the burn of 4's
before the double bell ends the day
and buses exhale beyond
the unopenable windows.
Eyes swallow
fluorescence and glow
a little green in the late
afternoon gloom, the faces closed
like Venetian blinds
though someone, perhaps
Ramón, whispers a slant
of light into the shadows
and Anthony catches the flame
like a sword to swallow,
a ruler slicing whatever luminescence
is left from air so used and wet
with breath it hardly holds the sky in place,
a fleck or two of blue
in a little boy's hair.

Black Mule

To be awakened by moonlight.
To be taken from suffering.

    To be carried to a night so blue and deep
        it seals the wounds.

To hear the salt of healing like the boil of waves retreating.

    To change the words to another song, to just one song, to
every song.

To feel daylight leave the earth like a yellow wind.
           To feel darkness turn silver in the veins.

To leave a trace like frost on the lip of a cup.
To know we are remembered.

To lose every fingerprint in the dust of an abandoned city.

To ride a black mule through rain and night and coal and ash
    and on into an emptying of air and light
    into hills blown brown and low and crumbling
    into the sea of a north coast summer.

    To ride on changed by being remembered.

      To change the words as if we could be remembered.

To stop too soon as if to turn
    to hear another voice at the edge of the clearing.

    To leave a trace
      like a fingerprint on the wind.

To heal into death like a song sung softly to a child at the edge
of sleep, who will remember it like the dream
of a father returning, his hands holding salt
to heal the forgetting, to heal every changed word.

Gypsy Hollow

What gypsy finds her way to West Virginia?
And is her family hidden at the edge
of town in camo tents pushed back beneath
the hemlocks, the bright scarves and braided chains
stuffed out of sight in sleeping bags and sacks
of sludge-colored burlap? Are they waiting?

She's cleared the sidewalk in front of City Hall
of competition, the one-word man ("Change?")
and his sombrero banished or worse, the beard
with a body who wears a boom box on
his shoulder somewhere else, perhaps the river
north of Shangri-La, which is, as always,

west of Everywhere, West Virginia. She's
selling paintings of parrots and men in
tams and fezzes, Aimé Césaire and
Léopold Senghor or someone equally
revolutionary, though not Marley
or Mutabaruka, not dub poets

or slam poets, though one looks a little
like a black John Clare, for whom a mount
in Harrison County is named. I watch
her snatch a twenty from a man's open
wallet: he was offering ten for a triptych
of birds found near or on an equator

she's never straddled, though she's holding her
own Maginot as cars honk past and passers-
by laugh. And now she's screaming, her back
to him who wants his money back but doesn't
need the scene he's suddenly part of. She's
packing up her canvases, dragging daylight

from the sky, still muttering in bursts,
still pointing wildly at anyone
close enough to see a flare rise in her eyes
like a sunbeam broken by a windowpane,
the heat an idea that almost burns,
like coal, which almost belongs to West Virginia,

the nothing that was that now stokes fires
in steam plants all over America,
the miners who wake in darkness deep
beneath the hollow and then become the darkness.
Why a gypsy in West Virginia,
in a hemlock forest pulling hamburgers

from a greasy white bag for her children,
cold hamburgers gone sour on her walk
from town? She's hidden her paintings beneath
a trestle that once bridged a creek for coal
trains heading to Pittsburgh along the river,
and now bears footsteps of joggers and after

dinner perambulators, who would never think
to look beneath their feet for beauty
however strange or cheap or stolen from
Rastas on Canal Street, who still wonder
where the fucking gypsy and her mean brood
have gone, who sing, *Who paints the prophet should*

profit as they roast pigeons over trash
cans filled with fire. Who steals the sun must lead
the children through a dusk the length of days.
She's pulling scarves from her sleeves to make room
for twenty dollar bills and a little
more light. We're all wondering where she's gone.

The Clock

We sit by the window
waiting for wine and watch
a car burn on Boundary Street,
a stopped clock above
the bar: half-past three
forever, and then it's now.
I remember a shady spot
north of here on I-5
called Crow's Landing
as five of them settle
on the line above the fire.
An Impala, I think,
or the newer Malibu.
They hop in the heat
waiting for the flames
to settle into smolder.
There's something to pick at
or they wouldn't be here.
And the INS guys in their
black Suburban. Just waiting.
Here at last, a gentle Lambrusco.
Half-past three with a view
of Boundary Street. Somewhere
behind us, Mexico. Eight
crows now, the fire nearly out.

Making Up for Lost Time

When last I looked is as good
as it gets, as good
as *broken moonlight* or the lost
earrings beneath a flower pot, a once-lost

key too small to fit the gate lock
or the antique roller skate, the lock
on the strong box, the trigger lock within.
When last I looked the doll within

the doll was chipped and cracked
like a ceiling by Giotto, a cracked
cup glued back together by a child
repairing her first broken cup, a child

so used to the magic words, *When last
I looked,* that she's found her mother's earrings, at last.

March 17th

Walt wore green trousers to school today,
a little tattered and short but baggy enough
to get by, his ankles sharp wings above
his shoes, Hermes delivering his little
sister to kindergarten, who's in a green cardigan
over green t-shirt; she hates to be pinched.
She isn't sure her classmates will eat
the guacamole we made this morning
for Green Tasting Day, and Amber, *of course*,
is bringing green popcorn. I mention snakes
and pagans, an island as green as the Hulk,
but they look at me as if my hair is on fire,
a peat fire in late winter, a cache of flames above
my ears. When St. Patrick left home a slave,
a stolen child in the service of thieves, the fairies
discerned a narrow faith and let him be,
let him labor and escape. If only leprechauns
possessed a missionary instinct. If only
they'd kept him in a bower counting shades
of green. If seen now in these days of Falwell
and Robertson, if found beneath a garden stone
or taking shelter in the heather, the little
people are menacing and mean, as apt
to boil a child as enchant him. Driven
underground by Patrick's return, they await
a different rapture, or the same one differently,
happy enough with an eternity bound over
to the earth, the smear of chlorophyll on their
cheeks as they walk among the heathens,
who believe what they see and little else.
The fairies require no one's belief.
The leprechauns play tricks on the damned
or the saved. Patrick taught the trinity
by counting the leaves on a shamrock, how
three things could be as one, then handing it
to a druid to hold, to consider. So when,

after school, Phoebe announces that, yes,
everyone loved the guacamole, and Walt
hands out his paper shamrocks inscribed
with messages, I think of spring, three days
away, which this year falls on Palm Sunday,
the day Walt was born eight years ago.
Did a nurse give me the small cross of bent
fronds or did I find it under his pillow,
right next to a four-leaf clover, a gift from
an uncle who has never believed, though he took
the time to search in his yard for a present.
Faith and luck: one found everywhere,
the other as rare as air at the bottom of the sea.
Both are in his baby book, right next
to a footprint and a bracelet that reads
Baby Boy Harms. Right now he wants
to eat the green cupcake his teacher passed
around before the final bell. Phoebe is
looking out the window counting clouds
aloud in Spanish, which means there
can only be ten. Ten clouds in the sky,
though from where I sit, there are hundreds.

You the Overheard

Still striking the hard horizon, the storm

sparks and sizzles, the smell of lead and wet wire.

First sails appear like handkerchiefs sopping up the bay

and someone speaks through the window of wet

afternoon air: "Just look at that."

The bluff above the sea. The white Adirondack chairs.

Someone says: "It's like an anvil, God's hammer."

The outdoor bar unrolls its awning.

Wine and a bowl of olives, your sister's trick:

a Sevillano on each finger, pimentos scattered

in the grass. The wet grass. The chairs bubbling with rain.

"I'm not sure I can stand here forever," someone says.

"So sit." The bell of crystal touching crystal.

No whales in this weather, though that's why

we've come. "God's hammer," he says again.

The storm pulses, a gray heart shot through with light.

She says, "The chairs are wet, this skirt is linen." And you,

overheard: *I'd like it to stop; if it would all please stop,*

though you're watching the sails, all this evidence of joy.

You've dropped your wineglass in the grass.

Providence

Why didn't I
when I saw you
say What
happened? Is it
you? Why
in the woods
beyond the wall
your father
stacked from stones
he found rolling
in the slow river
did snow seem
to pause in the pines
before sifting
to earth, to where
you sat in your
daughter's anorak
counting sounds
as they slipped
past. You knew
in your wonder
and your new coat
of sifted snow
that no one
would let you
go so easily as
I did once
when the world, at least
for us, was new
and blue
as smoke above the sea,
as your hands
there beneath
the trees without

mittens or my
hands
or anyone's breath
blowing blood back
to the fingertips.
Are you sure
you're safe now,
safe in arms of all
you need, providence?

Keep My Word (Aubade by Grant McLennan)

At dawn the third
dimension gradually returns,
a scent like salt
in the wind. The ocean
is a sound at the edge
of sleep, easily mistaken
for leaves gathering in
the courtyard corners,
and the leading edge
of light slips loose of
palm trees and jacaranda,
rattles like dice on the terra-
cotta tiles. At dawn I see
you best from the doorway,
your hair a nest in the gray air,
face closing already
as you draw the curtains
and return to bed.
I have friends who can list
the different herbs they smell
in a sauce, can grade
the sedimented soil in a sip
of wine, the vineyard's
long story of loam.
At dawn, colors begin
their slow return,
give weight to wind
and peel shadows into
shavings of night.
I will return is the promise
dawn completes, *return*
the word kept. The light
is full of water, water heavy
with reflected light.
The scar beside your eye
ripples as you sleep

like a narrow puddle brushed
by a breeze. At dawn, night
and day nearly blend, nearly
erase all differences, a way of
celebrating gray and
the end of gray, of saying
here and now are enough.
But here and now are made
entirely of two things,
hope and loss, though at dawn
they seem to touch.

TWO

Antarctica Starts Here

We never spoke
though I'm sure we met,
late winter light
frosting her strangely
brown hair (wrapped close
in Hermès, the only
concession to disguise).
She held with two fingers
her white Chanel
sunglasses, lifting them
now and then to chew
softly on an arm,
staring hard at
Bathers by a River.
Anyone could see
it was her, though
no one else did.
We loved the same
paintings I like to think,
O'Keefe's *Sky Above Clouds*,
Nighthawks of course,
and we took the same
time in each gallery.
After a few hours she
turned and nodded
thanks, and left—
no entourage or
bodyguard, no one
even to carry the bag
of books she bought
in the gift shop.
Did I volunteer
to help? Did I say,
in passing, as I held
the door open to

Michigan Avenue
with one hand, the bag
of books in the other,
that if I were given just
one meal and one
movie to end
my last day on earth,
I would go hungry and ask
for both *Belle du Jour*
and *Le Dernier Metro*?
I watched her
walk away beneath
the "lights that reach
from Barbary to here"
and felt the air return
to normal in my lungs,
though for hours
I smelled her perfume
in my shirt whenever
I lifted a sleeve
to my face, her *own*
perfume as it turned out:
she was in town
to debut *Deneuve,*
"a fragrance as chic
as its namesake"
I read in the *Tribune*
the next day, alongside
a note in the gossip column:
"Two hundred roses
delivered to Catherine
Deneuve's suite
at the Drake." But
I knew that.

Cary Grant

You know, I have about the same interest in jewelry
that I have in politics, horseracing, modern poetry,
or women who need weird excitement: none.
—JOHN ROBIE, *TO CATCH A THIEF*

The last time I saw Cary Grant, he was tearing apart bread
at the marina, a cloud of gulls around him. He let me
try on his glasses, those heavy black specs he wore
toward the end, and I bought a pair just like them,
though I didn't look like Cary Grant, so I went back to not trying.

The night before he died, Cary called from Iowa to talk,
just to talk. He said about David Niven: "He never
wore blue out of doors though every pair of pajamas
was a different shade of sky." When his voice dropped
I thought a flock of sparrows had landed all at once
somewhere on the line between Davenport and Los Angeles.

"Sometimes," he said, "David held my hand while we talked
over coffee, while we smoked on his patio; he had a lovely
pink house on Amalfi Drive. Sometimes we just sat there
watching the gardener prune the bougainvillea, listening
to traffic on Sunset Boulevard. It was as if only half
of what he was saying could be put into words."

Cary was quiet a while before he said, "Goodnight, my dear."
I sat without hanging up and listened to the dial tone, waiting
for the sparrows to lift, to go find another voice. What did
Dudley say to the Bishop at the end, a little wistfully
as he watched the window for a last look at Julia?
"I want to be far, far away from here."

Away from what, I've always wondered, though that's the half
that can't be said: a dial tone, a hush, a blue hum in a sky
filled with gulls. I didn't ask for his glasses that morning
at the marina, he just handed them over. "Wait till you see
what I see," he said. And he held my hand while I looked.

So Long, Sunset Boulevard

Red Foxx (is he still alive?) and I shared
a friend who ended up
as strung out as a pair of boxers
on a nice day in West Virginia, the traffic
along Route 50 lifting just enough breeze
to air out the underwear,
who started as a dealer and paid his mother's
rent and kept his brother
in private schools until he was old enough
to know enough
then ducked into the leaves and never said so long
to anyone, not to to his best friend who ended up
I wish I knew, he was my friend, too,
not to Hollywood and the easy marks, all those
tourists to Junkieland ready for
anything wrapped in foil, not to Highland
and Las Palmas and Wilcox and Vine,
all the cross streets west of Gower,
not to here and here's the rub:
he never said so long to Sunset Boulevard,
which has a way of seeming endless as it winds
toward the Pacific, where anyone
can end up out of road and alone
in the crowd above the sea, where
anyone can stand on the bluffs and watch
the ironic sunset, the air alive with ozone, with all
the parts per million, the grenadine pink
and safety vest orange, where Red Foxx
if he's still alive sips coffee
at a picnic table near
the phone booths, our friend
waiting, his hand

on a receiver and thinking about
what's next: a meeting with
his brother's teacher, a date with his
mother's gutters (all that clutter and sag),
but for now the waiting around for
a sound at sunset, the wind
in a dropped bottle, the sizzle
of waves drawing back, a bell above
the traffic, a chance to say
Hey and how much, to say OK and so long.

The Shield (of Captain America)

The two guys with do-rags
at the next table or whatever
they call them are pretending
not to care. I suppose this first
fall rain is a Joyce scholar's version
of source code, the frequency
of drivel in a coffee shop confession:
here's Lucy with an idea for Harriet,
who wonders what to do with
last night's roast, most of which
is in the crisper with half an onion
and a happy meal. I believe
in the sixteen action figures
lining the windowsills, particularly
Aquaman who is now called
Sharkboy, who exists for me
in the intersection of sunbeams
and a crooked nose . . .
did Reggie really break it
smelling his first wife's last dinner,
which she left boiling on the stove
like noise filling an empty head?
I believe she believed in
appropriate visions, which begin
in the coil of smoke above
a Pismo shell, the way the clouds
part to reveal a bruise: it's time
to run: she'll be back for her kit bag
of cosmetic samples midweek
next February while Reggie
is at work. Do-rags indeed.
They're talking interest rates

and rental properties. A feather
blows in with a rust (oops, gust) of rain
and Dorothy, whose hair is leaning east
and is the color of pureed carrots,
who's holding the plastic handles
of a wet paper sack. There goes
the bottom, the coffee shop filling with
plastic combs she sells from the bench
beside the Dairy Queen. Particularly
Captain America I meant to say,
who's back as bad as ever, silver shield
like a flat-screen T.V. in the broken
morning sunlight *where the altar
should have been*, the way raindrops
plump with heat as they fall in pieces
in the streets of this town, this
walled city on the verge of
coal field and mountaintop,
glorified on the good Captain's
shining shield, where all of us
see the text of the future. "Hello,
Hector," said Achilles. "Away we go."

Murmur R.E.M.

Kudzu on the cover. A song
wrapped in wax paper, all stammer and prayer
and the low, little sounds
of bugs scratching screens.
How many happy fools
in the meantime were wondering
at the edges, lament
disguised as barn owls
pitching their poor question
to the dark? And pity our
Angeline in her swamp-colored dress,
her feckless gardening
through the night.
Outside the moral kiosk
what starts as rain
ends up a voice in a tin cup,
a slur of doves
answering the ring of children
singing on the lawn.
What starts as dusk
turns into candle hum and sizzle,
the sprinkler watering
the neighbor's porch.
A radio buried in the wet dirt.

In Your Bright Ray

I haven't always loved the word guitar,
though two guitars in one song, like two trains
heading together toward Toledo or Akron
or some other city in Ohio, two trains on separate tracks,
one angling north to miss Columbus, where Union Station
disappeared into the dirt in 1976, the other ghosting I-70,
two trains traveling west but differently, one acoustic
and one electric with a violin filling in the shadows,
the electric losing its hold on notes as it moves north,
fuzzing around the edges, the acoustic as steady and straight
as a locomotive pulling into Union Station (if it were still there)
dragging a load of textiles, bolts of bright cloth for the new
industry of central Ohio, where light falls now unrefracted
by filth and fills the fields at dawn with shine . . .
or, for the poets of Cleveland, who have never gotten over
the clean air, with broken glass flashing in the grass . . .
two trains. But I believe now "In Your Bright Ray" has three
    guitars
and no violin, though two seem to be traveling the same track.
I have seen all the cities of Ohio, all the capitals of Europe,
but I've never been to Brisbane, though I love the name
(which is pronounced like "Has been," though I have not).
I hear the sunlight is striped in Brisbane and makes a sound
like a scar, which is to say like a voice that isn't there anymore,
    but is.

Lynda (Singing Chet Baker, 1988)

After surviving, what arrives?
Some phrases are eighth notes,
some trills, frost on the lawn, a flint
of moonlight in the grass.
Others sweeten breath
like blue noise in the deeper shade.
Like the jeweled beret she found
in a Little Rock thrift store,
the beer in her voice: I saw
streetlight through the tips
of her fingernails, the way
she stood slack-armed at
the window fronting High
Street: neon and gas lamp,
the elementary sadness
of downtown lights.
Let's get lost, she said—
we don't need to start
remembering until tomorrow.
All ascent takes the shape
of smoke leaving the body,
the body losing its shape.
To burn a word is a sin
unless it's still in someone's
throat. In the backseat
of Aleda's convertible
the music seemed wrapped
in a flapping flag, torn
and muffled, though the sound
of a blown-apart embouchure
and a junkie's croon
were reassembled in the wind
by her voice singing along.

It's OK if He's a Girl

–Rickie Lee Jones

I've never had wings
but I know what it's like to lose them.

The careful spot, the soft
place beneath a sleeve
of light bouncing off the tabletop:
not a bruise or a birthmark: an X:

That's where it hurts.

She named her Luke before she knew
but she knew. And Bird wasn't there
to say *Well there you go.*

And Bird wasn't there to say
Here's a picture of me in kindergarten.

They thought he was going for a gun
and poof: Bird wasn't there:

I write the dates on the back of anything
except my eyelids: 1979-2005: a bookie's receipt,
my hand, a little wallet picture.

This is not a test, but if
you name her Luke she's certain
to hate you, though it's not
the sort of hate that looks like a gun
and acts like a wallet.

"Bye-bye, Bird," you said to a door in the wall.
"Bye-bye, Black Bird."

Lost and Through

after Willy Vlautin

A casino lights the snow
a sort of blue as a bookie watches
the side door from his Buick
for my cousin, who's laughing
with my sister all curled up
under a blanket in the backseat
of our Sentra (we take turns
riding the bus). I pull up slow
until I'm even with his window,
then roll away mine, though it's
ten degrees in Reno, new snow
melting on the hood and turning
silver in the light, new snow
lying down on two feet of old
in the darkness beyond the casino's
blue glow. Before I hand him
the envelope of twenties, I write
my cousin's name on the front,
Fuck you across the seal.
You could say I'm saving his life
though the way he's laughing
he's just liking my sister's bad joke
about the blind Friar taking
confession from a castrato,
the castrato lately taken with barbells.
We're not lost sons my cousin and me,
though our fathers are brothers
in misery and shame and he's sick
of the inheritance. *Save my life*
he said this morning over coffee
and cigarettes. My sister works
in the dress store on Fourth Street
so it's her money, but I'm the one
driving and tomorrow I'll be driving

and we'll all of us, all three of us
change our clothes in a public restroom
in Redondo Beach and wait out
the night at a Denny's near the pier.
Next day we'll send postcards
we bought in Florida last April
to our fathers and hope they're too drunk
to notice the postmark. Not like
they're coming for us. But knowing
where we are is like giving them
a choice and it's our choice now: and we're
lost and through and saved and gone.

Range Life

after Pavement

A dappled mare in the center of Main Street. Wow, somebody says. Somebody says, *Would you look at that.* The lunch crowd spills from the diner buttoning jackets, carrying the last few bites of bologna sandwiches, cheese sandwiches, napkins still tucked in their shirts; they form a line along the curb, spectators at a modest parade. But nothing happens. She shakes her mane. A car beeps hello, its driver half out the window grinning stupidly. The mare walks shyly, like someone taught to walk with a book on her head, someone who suddenly can't feel the book. She spots a young boy eating candy, nuzzles his coat pocket; he pulls out a roll of lifesavers. The mare picks it gently off his palm, eats the candy, paper and all. And for once the fire truck arrives quietly, sirens swallowed like a sob. It must be over now, time to go, everyone waves. Sometimes waving "so long" is better than saying it, since the wave fades from sight without vanishing—the mare being led down an alley—lingers almost, a taste recurring through the day, the mayonnaise most likely, or a flavor buried in the salad dressing: garlic or thyme. And it's back to work, back to school—there's nothing to see here, folks, let's move on, though in the middle of the road is a steaming pile of shit, cars slowing, weaving slightly around it, flies gathering, the call being made. Like waving so long instead of saying it, someone calls in the report: there's shit in the street. OK, that's fine, we'll get right on it, but when they do it's gone, just cars and the unemployed, a few senior citizens pointing at the macadam, and the boy inching his head into the empty space an alley makes between buildings. Of course he's truant, dragged away, reported, given absolutely no credit for bringing off the day, and finally, as if to say there really isn't a life possible here, he's given a tour of the glue factory. Who could blame him for leaving? After all, school's out in a week. And somewhere there's a range life, a way of staying still, a silence. A permanent wave.

The Astronaut

It was sad about the astronaut.
But it's always sad to watch

the capsule fill with water,
to take the call and listen
to the colors of sea foam
and cephalopod described

from the inside. She never
gave up, he said. With all
that water in her throat.

In the thick air at fifty fathoms.
The barnacles and sea worms,

her face, the slow changes,
and her voice like a bubble
trapped in a bottle. "It's me,"

she said, though all we wanted
was to hear how it seemed

from space. And the fall. How
did it feel to fall so far?

Bachelor Kisses

1987-2007 (from Vinyl to iPod)

Peter was teaching at Oberlin, Karen
marrying for the first time in Chicago, and Lisa
offered a ride to the wedding, though we had
to stop in Ohio first to see old friends of hers (one
named Siegfried, believe it or not); halfway
to Oxford we pulled over to kiss, so I'm wondering
where was Kim?
        Lisa dropped me off
on her way back to Indiana and I waved
goodbye in the driveway before knocking
at Peter's sublet: three bedrooms and a sunken
den filled with bookshelves, the shelves themselves
filled with records, Stephanie already there
from Toronto: she found it first,
              though first
we shopped for turkey and four side dishes
from the Tuesday *New York Times:* dessert
was chocolate silk pie, a memory of Stephanie's
translated into cups and tablespoons.
The only turkey left
        in Oberlin on the Wednesday
before Thanksgiving weighed 25 pounds and was dead
just 24 hours. But the three of us had a week of sandwiches
to fill so we bought it
        and spread the paper on the kitchen table,
drank Canandaigua wines and listened to Stephanie's
"find" sixteen times in one day: *Spring Hill Fair*
by The Go-Betweens. "Bachelor Kisses"
was Peter's favorite track. Mine too.
        Stephanie blew up
balloons and taped them everywhere,
even her hair, mine too. Alan called from Tokyo
before dinner to talk to Peter, and I answered
saying, "Sherwood Forest, Robin Hood speaking."

I could tell by his voice he wasn't coming home,
though I never said a thing to Peter. We sang between
bites of our newspaper recipes:
                    Don't believe
what you've heard, faithful is not a bad word.
Elsewhere in the *Times*: news, box scores,
a book review, though not of one of ours. Peter read
"Slowly" out loud after dinner, still my favorite of all
his stories. *The New Yorker* bought it a month later
and we went to The Odeon to celebrate, though that
was a month later.
                    Oberlin. Thanksgiving. 1987.
By the end of the day I knew every word
of "Bachelor Kisses," and by now I know every
song he wrote. But does a song run out of time
or just the boy who wrote it, who believed in what
he sang until he stopped?
                    This poem is about to stop, too,
though here I am, standing up and singing where I
shouldn't be, not a shower in sight, the whole coffee shop
looking at me—
                    they know I'm not kidding.
Sometimes I think no one is listening except
these strangers wondering what to do, how to bag me up
and drag me off. I sit down and dial up the song again:
Hey wait, O please wait, don't rush off, you won't be late,
and then I realize hold on:
                    I'm listening: singing along
is a sort of listening, a way of saying to the silence
in every shadow, at the edges of every moment, at the center
of every song or poem or phone call from Tokyo . . . a way
        of saying,
"Silence, I hear you and I don't care: not now, not today."
        I'm listening
and I have been for twenty years.
                    And I'll keep listening until I stop.

Though Not about Him or for Him, a Poem Called Bill Murray

The truth about
Groundhog Day has nothing to do
with winter, nothing to do
with overcast mornings or the way
a shadow softens at the edges
like a child's first brush
with watercolor.
It has nothing to do with courage,
since even an eagle will balk
and falter when surprised
by its own shadow, the clouds
cracking just a bit as it drops
toward the rabbit, a shaft
of light and his shape
on the grass: black wings, black
talons, what's that?!:
the rabbit down the hole.
The truth about Groundhog Day
has nothing to do with weeks
of winter, with all the weariness
of watching the gray of another
dawn. A little boy turns
to his father and says, I hope
he sees his shadow and his father
says, I hope not, though he knows
they are hoping the same thing
since both of them, this second,
are collecting coal for the snowman's
eyes and buttons and love
these days when everything
is closed or canceled. Does
Santa Claus really bring coal
for bad children, says the boy . . .
but that's another poem,
a poem called Jimmy Stewart.

First Day of Spring (The Day My Eyes Came Back)

There are three songs in her hand. The orange
tastes like a hoofprint. First days are velvet slippers
in the trees, all these worms in an old soup can,
river of solder, river of twine. The river holds the earth
in place as it spins loose its loose leaves. I'm tired
of budding into air too clear to swallow. The day my eyes
came back she walked through the door like a blue shout
in the silver dusk. "I've still got your venom in my mouth."
She held my kiss beneath her tongue, touched my neck,
found the cobweb in my voice and brushed it loose.
"Don't bruise your knees," the one song goes. Please.

Trapped

When Jimmy Cliff sang "Trapped" I had never been
enough in love to wear chains, to give away
the three or four things I do well for the sake

of someone else's slim measure: I mean joy
as a feather on the scales, the weight of a cape
slipping off the shoulders. But whose cape?

This is when Dean would run for the river banging
a pan with a pistol and fingering the right wrist
for a pulse or a tattoo of Singapore, the whole city

on his forearm, though neither of us cared for
the blue aleph of "everyness" those years between stations.
And Dean would never say *Borges* while I

can't seem to stop dropping names.
"I will teach my eyes to see beyond these walls
in front of me," though even the metaphor

in the metaphysics is a sort of loofah on a stick,
a sponge I could have eaten had I been there
at the harvest. It wasn't Dean nor was it David

who worried metaphor was simply evasion,
though here I go, as far from chains as a retired jailer.
Clemency has nothing to do with guilt or, as it

turns out, innocence. But I'm sick of mercy.
Or maybe just tired of it, tired of asking at the end
of the day for the quiet inside a seashell, which is

to say for music as it simmers down. And there it is:
from Jimmy Cliff to Bob Marley in a phrase.
What better way to slip away, to break away,

to end away from where I started: trapped.

Another

No one needs another ghost story
except my son, who waits hard
outside the door to dreams to hear
mine all the way through. What
room, what house, will he remember
as his first? Which ghost? I woke
each night for weeks to find my
grandfather watching, sitting at the foot
of my bed waiting for my eyes to open.
He never spoke, just shifted away
from the streetlight falling through
the window, his face dissolving
into shadow like a photograph
dropped in a puddle. Sometimes
his glasses caught the light and turned
to white, his eyes vanishing for long
seconds until his head turned again
toward a sound at the door, my mother
come to check on me, his daughter
wondering how I was, wondering
if somehow he was really back.
She told me once she saw him too.
I tell my son, It's true, it's true, though
he's given up, is sleeping west of
anywhere. Outside, a crescent moon
is pasted to the night sky like a scar
on a little boy's suntanned cheek.
I touch it as he sleeps, believing all
I can feel or see or remember.

A Wooden Horse

"Oh bring it in and let us see it."
—BSP

We tied ropes and pulled.
It rolled a little, and then enough
to cross the drawbridge,
which we drew back shut and locked
with iron rods. Nick and Sally
climbed the tower and crouched
low behind the parapet to take
their turns watching the east,
from whence cometh nearly
everyone we've ever hated.
We'd heard the rumors and
knocked. But the thing was
all echoey and empty, though
inside we found flowers
and enough red wine to
tip the town into dreams
of poppies and fair
weather. Salvador sang
"The Ballad of Queenie
and Rover" while Ted sliced
the ham and spread mustard
on bread, and Evangeline
for once let down her black
braid and taught the kids
the cha-cha. We were ready
when they charged, daisies
behind our ears. "Whosoever
steals will be blinded," Jamal
cried, as if reading from
the dictionary. Salvador
kept singing and we offered
the immigrants leftover
salad and what little

ham remained. "It was better
before we were barbarians,"
Franny whispered.
But they'd given us the wine
and wrapped it in wood,
and sent us a hollow horse
to hold our dreams in case
our hearts, at last, were full.

Comet Scar

For months after his death
Phoebe sings along
in the backseat
to "Comet Scar"
without a word
except the words
to the song. Then,
one day, she asks
"What's a comet scar?"
and I say it's what's left
from coming so far,
a scar on a girl
who "knows more
than ordinary people
ever know."
But those are just
the lyrics and she's
already heard them,
though she doesn't argue.
Now she's singing
"One Plus One,"
which doesn't require
explanations since
"One plus one equals two,"
she says, and she's sure.
But two ones never add up
to anything in the song,
which is about love
and its aftermath,
and some day she'll ask
about that. Maybe
it will be the day she says
"Who's singing" and I'll
tell her. And as always
she'll follow up with
"Is he alive or dead,"

which she gets from
her older brother, who's
not happy that Basil
Rathbone is no longer
with us and checks
nearly every day to see
if Johnny Depp is still
around. Film is tricky that way.
So I guess I'll tell her, "No,
he's not alive,"
though instead, perhaps,
we'll listen to "Finding You,"
his last AM hit, where he asks
"What would you do
if you turned around
and saw me beside you,
not in a dream but in a song?"
And without looking
in the rearview mirror
I'll say, "Can you see him
beside you, Phoebes?"
and I know she'll say
yes because she believes
in all sorts of things
she can't see, which is
a kind of seeing. And while
the song is playing
and maybe longer
we'll both sing along,
which is a kind of seeing.

Lamp by Lamp

A single surfer
drifts between
pilings and
paddles out
the pier's south side,
dusk dissolving
into darkness.
Before long the moon
through clouds
marks footsteps
on the sea.
Each summer
a little earlier
the water warms
and thickens
with dying kelp,
the wrack of August
in July. Pilot whales
lost on their way
shine with moonlight,
footsteps heading
north lamp by lamp
and too soon.

Notes

"My Life in Art" is after the song of the same title by Mojave 3.

"Friday Rich/Saturday Poor" takes its title from a song by The Apartments.

"Flags" lists several titles by the following artists, in order: Miles Davis, Paul Kelly, Chris Isaak (not Ryan Adams, though his is good too), X, New Order, Ryan Adams.

"Or Two Cans Tied Together with String" borrows and quotes from The Felice Brothers.

"Satie" is for Tony Hoagland and makes reference to Belle & Sebastian.

"Song of Sand, Song of Sea, Song of Leaving, Song of Leaves" is for Christopher Buckley. The song referred to in this poem, "Here Comes a Regular," is by Paul Westerberg and was performed by The Replacements.

"You the Overheard" was inspired by a line by Peter Makuck.

"Antarctica Starts Here" takes its title and quotes from the song by John Cale.

"In Your Bright Ray" borrows its first line from David St. John, with thanks for everything.

"Lynda (Singing Chet Baker, 1988)" is in memory of two dear friends, Lynda Hull and Aleda Shirley.

"The Astronaut" is for Brian Henry.

"Bachelor Kisses" is for Peter Cameron.

"Trapped" is for Dean Young.

"A Wooden Horse" was inspired by British Sea Power and includes a reference to Paul Kelly's "The Ballad of Queenie & Rover."

For their help, support and friendship, my thanks to Jerry Costanzo, David Wojahn, John Hoppenthaler, Jeff Carpenter, Linda Warren and my students and colleagues at West Virginia University and New England College. And once again, to Aleda Shirley: "I wish I could feel people I love who are gone/with me still. They are not, and I can't."

For their endless inspiration: thank you, Walt, Phoebe, Grace and Dash.

ABOUT THE AUTHOR

James Harms is the author of seven previous books of poetry, including After West, *published by Carnegie Mellon University Press in 2008. His awards include a National Endowment for the Arts Fellowship, three Pushcart Prizes, and the PEN/Revson Fellowship. He lives with his wife, Amanda Cobb, and their children in Morgantown, West Virginia, where he teaches at West Virginia University. He also directs the low-residency MFA Program in Poetry at New England College.*

ABOUT THE BOOK

The text of Comet Scar *is set in Hightower (1994), designed by Tobias Frere-Jones, and Caecilia (1990), designed by Peter Matthias Noordzij. This book was designed by Linda Warren at Studio Deluxe, Culver City, California. It was printed and bound by Jeff Carpenter of Westcott Press, Altadena, California.*